Free time 1

She doesn't like playing the guitar.

Look. Then match and write.

1  a _____ reading the newspaper.

2  b _____ skateboarding.

3  c She doesn't like cooking.

4  d _____ playing computer games.

5  e _____ skiing.

6  f _____ playing the guitar.

7  g _____ watching TV.

1 What do you like doing?

Unscramble the questions and answers. Then draw.

1 Tom / what / doing / does / like

   Q: _What does Tom like doing?_

   computer games / likes / playing / he

   A: _____

2 what / Mum and Dad / like / doing / do

   Q: _____

   reading / they / like / the / newspaper

   A: _____

3 like / doing / Mary / what / does

   Q: _____

   likes / cooking / she

   A: _____

Read. Then circle.

1 *Do /* (*Does*) Sara like cooking? Yes, she does.

2 Does Tom like painting? No, he *don't / doesn't*.

3 Do they *like / likes* walking the dog? Yes, they do.

4 *Do / Does* you like skateboarding? Yes, I do.

5 Does she *like / likes* skipping? Yes, she does.

6 Do you like watching TV? Yes, I *do / does*.

Write.

1 Does Sara like playing   (Sara / play / hockey / ?)
  hockey?

2 Tom doesn't like reading   (Tom / read / the newspaper / ✗)
  the newspaper.

3 _____   (Sara / chat / online / ✔)

4 _____   (they / play / computer games / ✔)

5 _____   (we / watch / films / ✗)

Read. Then find two questions and answers.

What   you

  do

    like

doing

I   like

online   chatting

Do   your

  friends   playing

like   hockey

No   don't

  they

1 What do _____   2 _____

2 Wild animals
Do lions eat meat?

1 **Find the mistakes. Then correct.**

1 <u>Does</u> lions eat meat? <u>Do lions eat meat?</u>

2 They eats fruit. _____

3 Do elephants lives in forests? _____

4 Yes, they does. _____

5 Does hippos eat fruit? _____

6 Giraffes eating leaves. _____

2 **Read. Then circle.**

Orangutans [1](live)/ lives in the rainforest. They [2] have / are herbivores.
They [3] eat / eating a lot of fruit. They've [4] are / got very long arms and
they [5] likes / like climbing trees.

3 **Draw your favourite animal. Then write about what it eats and where it lives.**

_____

_____

_____

_____

Read and complete. Use words from the box.

What   ~~do~~   does   eat   lives   eats   live   Where

1 Where ___do___ giraffes live? They _____ in Africa.

2 _____ does a monkey live? It _____ in a forest.

3 What _____ a gorilla eat? It _____ fruit and leaves.

4 _____ do pandas eat? They _____ bamboo.

Read. Then unscramble and write.

1
animal / what's /
favourite / your

What's your favourite
animal?

My favourite animal
is the crocodile.

2
live / where /
crocodiles / do

_____

_____

They live in rivers.

3
what / they /
eat / do

_____

_____

They eat fish
and meat.

Read and match.

1 Giraffes eat
2 Crocodiles
3 Giraffes can run fast
4 Crocodiles have got

a swim quickly.
b a lot of leaves.
c 65 teeth.
d but they walk slowly.

Read. Then circle.

1 *How much /* How many *teeth have pandas got?*
They've got *much / a lot* – 42!

2 *How much / How many* meat do crocodiles eat?
They eat *much / a lot*.

3 *How much / How many* types of elephant are there?
There's / There are two types – African and Asian.

Read and complete. Use words from the box.

fast   slowly   ~~well~~   climb   walk   swim

1 Crocodiles swim _well_ .
2 Elephants _____ slowly.
3 Fish _____ fast.

4 Camels run _____ .
5 Monkeys _____ well.
6 Giraffes walk _____ but run fast.

The seasons

What's the weather like?

Read. Then match.

1 What's the weather like in spring?

a Sometimes it's wet and there's thunder and lightning. Other times it's warm.

2 What's the weather like in winter?

b It's hot and sunny. Sometimes it's humid.

3 What's the weather like in summer?

c It's cold and snowy.

Unscramble and write. Then draw.

1 windy / today / it's

It's windy today.

2 thunder / there's / and / lightning

3 winter / in / it's / snowy / very

4 today / 17 / degrees / it's

I go skiing in winter.

Look and read. Then write.

	Skiing	Hiking	Camping	Surfing	Cycling
Spring	Ben	Ben	Ben	Tom	Tom
Summer		Jo and Sue	Jo and Sue	Tom	Kim and Mark
Autumn		Kim and Mark	Tom		Ben
Winter	Ben				

1 Ben goes skiing in winter and spring. (*Ben / skiing*)

2 _____ (*Kim and Mark / hiking*)

3 _____ (*Tom / surfing*)

4 _____ (*Jo and Sue / camping*)

5 _____ (*Ben / cycling*)

6 _____ (*Tom / camping*)

Write about what you do in each season.

1 _____ (*spring*)

2 _____ (*summer*)

3 _____ (*autumn*)

4 _____ (*winter*)

Complete the sentences with *is* or *was*.

1 What ___is___ the temperature today?

2 What _____ the weather like yesterday?

3 It _____ sunny and warm today.

4 It _____ 25 degrees yesterday.

5 What _____ the weather like last winter?

6 It _____ 15 degrees today!

What was the weather like last winter? Look and write.

	November	December	January
Weather			
Temperature			

1 What was the weather like in November? _____ It was rainy.

2 What was the temperature in November? _____ It was 5 degrees.

3 _____ It was stormy.

4 _____ It was 2 degrees.

5 _____ It was 7 degrees.

6 _____ It was snowy.

4 My week

What do you do on Sundays?

1 **Complete. Then write the letter.**

> they practise have does ~~do~~ he

1 What _do_ you do on Sundays? | **d**

2 What do _____ do on Mondays? | ☐

3 What does _____ do on Wednesdays? | ☐

4 Does she _____ music lessons on Thursdays? | ☐

5 Does your friend _____ the piano on Sundays? | ☐

6 What _____ she do on Fridays? | ☐

a She learns to cook.

b Yes, she does.

c No, he doesn't.

d I learn to draw.

e He does gymnastics.

f They do karate.

2 **Answer about you.**

1 What do you do on Sundays?

_____

2 Do you study English on Mondays?

_____

Read the letter. Then circle.

Hi Jamie,
How are you? I've got a new timetable
this year. I ¹*has / have* piano lessons on
Wednesdays at half ²*past / to* three. I
³*do / does* my homework every day at four
o'clock. On Thursdays I do karate, and my
sister ⁴*practise / practises* the violin and
⁵*learns / practises* to draw. On Fridays
I play basketball after school.

What's your timetable like this year?
When ⁶*do / does* you have music lessons?
Write soon.
Liam.

Read again. Then write answers and questions.

1 When does Liam have piano lessons?

He has piano lessons Wednesdays at half past three.

2 When does he do homework?

_____

3 _____

She practises the violin and learns to draw on Thursdays.

4 _____

He plays basketball on Fridays after school.

4 always, never, often

Look and write sentences about Jo. Use *always*, *never* and *often*.

	Do homework		Have music lessons		Learn to cook		Study English	
	Jo	Me	Jo	Me	Jo	Me	Jo	Me
Mon	✔						✔	
Tues	✔				✔			
Wed	✔				✔		✔	
Thurs	✔				✔			
Fri	✔				✔		✔	
Sat	✔						✔	
Sun	✔							

1 Jo always does her homework. _____ (*do homework*)

2 _____ (*have music lessons*)

3 _____ (*learn to cook*)

4 _____ (*study English*)

Look at Activity 5 and complete the table about you. Then write sentences with *always*, *never* and *often*.

1 _____ (*do homework*)

2 _____ (*have music lessons*)

3 _____ (*learn to cook*)

4 _____ (*study English*)

Jobs 5

What do you want to be?

Unscramble the sentences. Then match.

1 to / player / be / basketball / I / a / want

   I want to be a basketball player.

2 don't / police / to / want / officer / be / I / a

3 astronaut / be / want / don't / to / an / I

4 a / want / film / to / star / be / I

a

b

c

d

Write the questions.

1 What does she want to be?

She wants to be a builder.

2 _____

I want to be a ballet dancer.

3 _____

He wants to be a lawyer.

Read. Then match.

1 Mary likes writing.   a   nurse

2 Pete likes running.   b   journalist

3 Julie likes helping people.   c   film stars

4 Roger likes working on cars.   d   ballet dancers

5 Sarah and Kim like dancing.   e   carpenter

6 Tim and John like acting.   f   mechanic

7 Carl likes making things.   g   athlete

Look at Activity 3. Write questions and answers.

1   **Does**   Mary **want to be** an athlete?

   No, she doesn't. She wants to be a journalist.

2 _____ Pete _____ an athlete?

3 _____ Julie _____ a nurse?

4 _____ Roger _____ a carpenter?

5 _____ Sarah and Kim _____ ballet dancers?

6 _____ Tim and John _____ journalists?

7 _____ Carl _____ a carpenter?

Read and complete. Use words from the box.

~~want~~   be   like   at   like   because   good   because

Ben

I ¹ **want** to be a journalist ²_____ I like talking to people and asking questions! I also ³_____ reading newspapers and magazines and I'm ⁴_____ at writing.

Sue

I want to ⁵_____ a builder ⁶_____ I like making things. I ⁷_____ drawing houses and bridges and I'm good ⁸_____ Maths.

Read. Then circle.

1 Why does Wendy (want) / wants to be a doctor? Because she likes *help / helping* people.

2 Why *do / does* he want to be a singer? Because he's *likes / good* at singing.

3 Do *you / he* want to be a farmer? Yes, I *do / does*.

4 *What / Why* do they want to be? They *want / wants* to be film stars.

What do you want to be and why? Write.

_____

_____

6 In the rainforest

The hut is near the river.

① Unscramble the sentences. Then write.

1 two mountains / there / behind / the rainforest / are

There are two mountains behind the rainforest.

2 a waterfall / between / the mountains / there's

_____

3 a river / there's / the rainforest / near

_____

4 a bridge / across / there's / the river

_____

5 huts / near / there / are / the bridge

_____

② Read your answers in Activity 1. Then draw the picture.

Look and read. Then write questions and answers.

	When little	Now
Tom	ski ✗	ski ✔
Sara	speak English ✔	speak English ✔
Jo and Sam	skateboard ✗	skateboard ✗
Kim and Mike	run ✔	run ✔

1 Could Tom ski when he was little?   No, he couldn't.

Can Tom ski now?   Yes, he can.

2

3

4

Complete about you. Then write.

When little	Now
✗	✔
✔	✔

When I was little, I could _____ but _____ .

Now I can _____ and _____ .

6 walk / walked

Read. Then circle.

1 I *walk / walked* to the shop yesterday.

2 They could *climb / climbed* trees when they were young.

3 She always *plays / played* football after school.

4 They *hike / hiked* last autumn.

5 Yesterday I *watch / watched* TV.

6 She *practises / practised* the piano every day at four o'clock.

Read. Then complete.

Last year I [1] **visited** (visit) New Forest. We [2]_____ (camp) in the forest. The weather [3]_____ (be) nice and we [4]_____ (walk) every day.

New Forest has got lots of horses. We [5]_____ (can go) near them but we [6]_____ (cannot give) them food. There [7]_____ (be) also lots of trees and some small lakes. We [8]_____ (can walk) around a big lake that [9]_____ (be) near our campsite. The campsite was great. Our trip [10]_____ (be) such fun!

Write about your last summer holiday.

_____

_____

_____

Feelings  7

Why are you smiling?

Read. Then write the letter.

1 Why are you crying? `d`

2 Why are you nervous?

3 Why are you laughing?

4 Why is your sister shouting?

5 Why is your mum blushing?

6 Why are you tired?

a Because there's a funny movie on TV.

b Because my grandad can't hear!

c Because she's embarrassed.

d Because I'm sad.

e Because I have a piano test.

f Because I walked to school.

Unscramble the questions and answers.

1 she / smiling / why / is

Q: Why is she smiling?

smiling / she's / because / birthday / it's / her

A: She's smiling because it's her birthday.

2 your / crying / why / is / brother

Q: _____

because / he's / crying / he's / hurt

A: _____

3 are / shaking / you / why

Q: _____

angry / I'm / because / I'm / shaking

A: _____

7 What's the matter?

Answer the questions.

1 What makes you feel embarrassed?

   Singing makes me feel embarrassed. (*sing*)

2 What makes you feel tired?

   _____ (*walk to school*)

3 What makes you feel relieved?

   _____ (*pass a test*)

4 What makes you feel proud?

   _____ (*play football well*)

Write the questions.

1 How do you feel? _____ I feel embarrassed.

2 _____ I'm sad.

3 _____ I feel tired.

Read. Then complete.

What's the matter?

I'm _____.

Why are you _____?

I'm _____ because _____.

Read. Then circle.

Dear Mum,

¹*I* / *Me* am having a great time with Aunt Sue and Uncle John. Aunt Sue gives ²*I* / *me* lots of little jobs to do. But they're fun jobs so it's OK. Uncle John is very funny. ³*He* / *Him* tells ⁴*we* / *us* funny stories about when ⁵*he* / *him* was a boy. They make me laugh.

Yesterday ⁶*we* / *us* visited a park and played football. It was so much fun.

Aunt Sue and Uncle John are terrific. I love staying with ⁷*they* / *them*.

Sarah

Match. Then write.

1 We don't understand.

2 The cat is thirsty.

3 It's his birthday.

4 Pick up the towels.

a Let's give _____ some cake.

b Put _____ in the cupboard.

c Give _____ some water.

d Can you help, __us__ ?

Unscramble and write. Then circle *T* (True) or *F* (False) about you.

1 teacher / hand / my / me / out / books / the / asks / never / to

   <u>My teacher never asks me to hand out the books.</u>   *T* / *F*

2 mum / gives / birthday / always / books / me / my / for / my

   _____   *T* / *F*

3 grandma / my / often / us / tells / stories / interesting

   _____   *T* / *F*

8 Action!

Let's go fishing!

1 Read. Then circle.

1 Let's go *snorkel* / (*snorkelling*)!
2 He doesn't like *water ski* / *water skiing*.
3 We're fond of *rafting* / *raft*.
4 I'm terrified of *scuba dive* / *scuba diving*.
5 They're crazy about *hang gliding* / *hang glide*.
6 You're really good at *surfing* / *surf*.

2 Complete the sentences with *of*, *about* or *with*.

1 I'm fond ___of___ skateboarding.
2 Tom's bored _____ rollerblading.
3 We're scared _____ bungee jumping.
4 Sara is terrified _____ singing in front of people.
5 I'm crazy _____ water skiing.
6 They're fond _____ scuba diving.

3 Write sentences about you.

1 _____ (*fond*)
2 _____ (*crazy*)
3 _____ (*bored*)
4 _____ (*scared*)
5 _____ (*terrified*)

Read. Then order the dialogue.

- [ ] Great idea! Have you got a surfboard?
- [ ] I'm not fond of kayaking. What about surfing?
- [ ] Hi, Ben. How are you?
- [ ] Let's go horse-riding!
- [1] Hi, Oli.
- [ ] Sorry, I'm terrified of horses. What about kayaking?
- [ ] I'm fine. What do you want to do today?
- [ ] My dad has got one. Let's go and ask.

Complete the conversation. Use the prompts.

Tomas: 1 _Let's go kayaking!_ _____ (let's / kayaking)

Freddy: 2 _____ (I / not good / kayaking)
    What about fishing?

Tomas: OK. 3 _____ (you / have got / fishing rod)

Freddy: Yes, I've got two.

Tomas: 4 _____ (you / be / fond of / fishing)

Freddy: Yes! 5 _____ (I / be / crazy about / fishing)

Tomas: OK! Let's go!

What are you going to do?

6 **Look and read. Then write questions and answers.**

	Next Monday	Next weekend	Next year
Tom	do English test	go horse-riding	visit Argentina
Sara	play guitar	play video games	go to new school

1 What's Tom going to do next Monday?

<u>He's going to do an English test.</u>

2 What's Sara going to do next Monday?

_____

3 What's Tom going to do next weekend?

_____

4 <u>What's Sara going to do next weekend?</u>

She's going to play video games.

5 _____

He's going to visit Argentina.

6 _____

She's going to go to a new school.

7 **Complete the chart about you. Then write sentences.**

	Next Monday	Next weekend	Next year
Me	_____	_____	_____

1 I'm going to _____ .

2 _____

3 _____